A CENTURY IN
THE COMPTROLLER'S OFFICE,
STATE OF NEW YORK, 1797 TO 1897

LECTOR HOUSE PUBLIC DOMAIN WORKS

A CENTURY IN THE COMPTROLLER'S OFFICE, STATE OF NEW YORK, 1797 TO 1897

JAMES ARTHUR ROBERTS

ISBN: 978-93-5420-870-6

Published: 1897

LECTOR HOUSE LLP
E-MAIL: lectorpublishing@gmail.com

Cornell Law School Library

**State Hall

A CENTURY IN THE COMPTROLLER'S OFFICE STATE OF NEW YORK

BY

JAMES A. ROBERTS

COMPTROLLER

1897

A CENTURY IN
THE COMPTROLLER'S OFFICE.

On the 17th of February, 1897, occurred the one hundredth anniversary of the establishment of the office of Comptroller of the State of New York.

The present incumbent of the office trusts it will not be considered unwarranted pride which has led him to collect and transcribe, in honor of its one hundredth birthday, such general facts relating more or less directly to the office, or to the former incumbents thereof, as he has gathered from unsystematic reading and in the performance of his duties.

An office which has without scandal managed the financial affairs of this great State, and has otherwise borne a conspicuous part in its government for a century; an office from the thirty incumbents of which have been chosen a Vice-President and a President of the United States, two United States Senators, four Governors of the State, one Chief Justice and one Chief Judge of its Court of Appeals—to say nothing of others who have achieved distinction in less conspicuous civil positions—would seem entitled to something more than a passing notice on its centennial anniversary.

The office, as created, and from time to time enlarged, is a unique feature in our State government. There are Auditors in nearly all of the States of the Union; but the duties of Comptroller are far broader, comprehending largely the ordinary duties of a State Treasurer as well as many others. There had been Auditors in the Colony of New York from 1680 down to the time of its organization as an independent State, and that office was continued in the State until it was merged in the office of Comptroller. There have been Treasurers of New York with varying duties from 1706 down to the present time. From the time of the organization of the State government the offices of Treasurer and Auditor had not been found to work harmoniously or satisfactorily. Bills might be audited which the Treasurer did not wish to pay, and the Treasurer might wish to pay bills which the Auditor would not pass, so in a tentative, experimental way in 1797 the office of Comptroller was created to combine the power to audit and the power to pay. The act creating it was framed by Samuel Jones, a man of note in his time (for whom Samuel Jones Tilden, the distinguished Governor of this State, was named), and on the 17th of February, 1797, it became law by the signature of that distinguished patriot, Governor John Jay.

The appointment of Comptroller upon the creation of the office fell to the "Council of Appointment," as was the case at that time with all State, county and municipal officers, except the Governor, Lieutenant-Governor and members of the Legislature. The "Council of Appointment" was an anomaly in government. The article (XXIII of the Constitution of 1777) establishing this "Council" was framed by three as pure, patriotic and disinterested statesmen as New York has ever produced, John Jay, Robert R. Livingston and Gouverneur Morris, and was designed to prevent a dangerous centralization of power in the hands of the Governor. It provided "that all officers, other than those who by this Constitution are directed to be otherwise appointed, shall be appointed in the manner following, to wit: The Assembly shall once in every year openly nominate and appoint one of the Senators from each great district" (then four in number), "which Senators shall form a council for the appointment of officers, of which the Governor, for the time being, or the Lieutenant-Governor, or the President of the Senate (when they shall respectively administer the government), shall be president, and have a casting vote, but no other vote."

Under the power thus conferred this council appointed the heads of the various State departments; all Judges, as well as Justices of the Peace, District Attorneys, Sheriffs, County Clerks, Mayors, and other officers throughout the entire State.

The cautious and anxious gentlemen who framed this provision in 1777 could by no means have foreseen the disastrous and disgraceful spoils system that grew up under it. It remained in full effect until a disgusted people abolished it by an amendment to the Constitution in 1821. At that time its power had so grown that there were 6,663 civil and 8,287 military offices which it controlled. The modern political boss must experience a feeling of profound regret as he realizes that this rich harvest can no longer be garnered by his sickle.

Chapter 21 of the Laws of 1797, which created the office of State Comptroller, provided, among other things, that "all matters and things theretofore required to be done by the Auditor of the State should be done by the Comptroller, and that the salary and wages of all legislative, executive, judicial and ministerial officers of the government of this State, and all moneys directed by law to be paid to any other person, should be paid by the Treasurer on the warrant of the Comptroller;" that the Comptroller should keep an account between the State and the Treasurer; that he might lend out moneys in the treasury not otherwise appropriated, and that when money was directed to be paid, and not sufficient money in the treasury to satisfy the same, he might "in the name, and on behalf of the People of this State, borrow a sum sufficient for that purpose of a bank of New York, or bank of Albany."

Thus the important powers which have distinguished the Comptroller's office—the power of audit; to draw warrants for all payments from the treasury; to keep its books of financial transactions; to invest its funds, and to borrow money—were embodied in the first act. The powers thus granted infringed so largely upon the ordinary rights and duties of a Treasurer, and so largely upon those which had been theretofore exercised by the Treasurer of this State, that it is not strange the then Treasurer, Gerardus Bancker, who had held the office from April 1, 1778, resigned in disgust. His feeling was, as Lossing has stated in his "Empire State," that the Comptroller was made "the highest financial officer of the State, and the Treasurer merely a clerk to him."

The early history of the office is an illustration of the cautious and doubtful temper of the Legislatures of the time—so unlike those of the present day. It is a well-known fact that while the Legislature of the State met for the first time at Albany, in the same year, 1797, in which the office of Comptroller was created, it was not then made a permanent location for the Capitol; and that city was maintained for upwards of twenty years as the Capitol simply by the adjournment of the Legislature at the end of each session to meet again at the city of Albany. The original act creating the Comptroller's office provided that it should continue in force for a period of three years. On the 28th day of February, 1800, eleven days after the office had expired by limitation, chapter 11 of that year went into effect, which re-established the office for another period of three years. Chapter 22 of the Laws of 1803 extended the office, with the powers and duties then prescribed by law, to February 28, 1805. By chapter 60 of the Laws of 1805, passed March 30th, the office was continued to February 28, 1808, and the acts of the then Comptroller, between the 28th day of February, 1805, and the day when this act went into effect, were ratified and confirmed. On March 11, 1808, chapter 34 of that year was passed, which continued the office to February 28, 1812, with a like confirmatory clause. The act of February 28, 1812, at last made permanent the Comptroller's office, with the powers theretofore conferred upon it. By chapter 31 of the Laws of 1797 the office of Comptroller was to be located either in Albany or Watervliet.

The Council of Appointment chose for the first Comptroller Samuel Jones, of Oyster Bay, Queens county. This was done by the casting vote of Governor John Jay, the four senatorial members of the council being a tie. He was a lawyer of high standing at the time of his appointment, a Federalist in politics, and had held with credit a number of civil positions. In 1775 he had been a member of the Provisional War Committee, and had performed arduous services on that committee. He was a member of the convention that adopted the Federal Constitution, and voted for it. He was a delegate to the Continental Congress in 1778; a Member of Assembly from Queens county in 1786, 1787, 1788, 1789 and 1790; a State Senator from the southern district from 1791 to 1799.

The honors which he had won and worthily worn were supplemented in his son who, as the Chancellor of this State (succeeding Nathan Sanford and succeeded by Reuben H. Walworth), and as Chief Judge of the New York Superior Court, won for himself enviable renown in our legal annals. Comptroller Jones was the author of the "Act for the amendment of law and better advancement of Justice," passed in 1789, which was a valuable contribution and addition to our law. He was also the author of many other of the best statutes placed upon our books in those early years. He was distinguished throughout his career as an upright and useful man, though he was sometimes accused of a little uncertainty in politics. He is said to have replied to a question from Judge Spencer as to how he managed to secure his elections from Queens county whatever party might be in the ascendant, that "If my troops will not follow me, I follow my troops."

The Comptroller's salary was fixed by the act at $3,000, and this was to include all clerk hire and ordinary expenses connected with the office. In 1800 the compensation was reduced to $2,500, and in consequence of this action Mr. Jones resigned the office. He had faithfully performed its duties, and his resignation terminated his public career.

During his term, in 1799, the Legislature prohibited the payment of any money from the treasury except upon the warrant of the Comptroller, and required all receipts to be countersigned by him, and this has remained a part of the duties of the Comptroller from that time to this.

On March 12, 1800, John V. Henry, an eminent Albany lawyer and a Federalist, was chosen Comptroller. There are some still living who know, at least by oral tradition, his great influence at the bar, and Albanians have a just pride in his high reputation. He was a member of the convention called in 1801 principally to settle the question whether the Governor alone could nominate persons for appointment, or whether that power also lay in the Senators composing the Council of Appointment. He was a Member of Assembly from Albany county in 1800, 1801 and 1802. During his term, by chapter 61 of the Laws of 1801, the Comptroller was made *ex-officio* a member of the State Board of Canvassers, and by chapter 69 of the same year he was made one of the Commissioners of the Land Office.

In 1801 the Legislature also directed the Comptroller to sell lands for the payment of taxes due to the State, and this power, variously modified and enlarged, still remains in him. Under it sales were held in 1808, 1811, 1812, 1814, 1815, 1821,

1826, 1830, 1834, 1839, 1843, 1848, 1853, 1859, 1866, 1871, 1877, 1881, 1885, 1890 and 1895.

In 1800 the Legislature authorized the Comptroller to settle the credits of the State with the Secretary of the Treasury of the United States. The moneys derived from this source formed the basis of the general fund. The Comptroller was made the custodian of this fund with power to invest it. The fund was augmented from sales of land and other sources until, in 1814, it had reached the sum of $4,396,943.97. The income of the fund together with the salt and auction duties, it was believed, in the early part of the century, would be sufficient to maintain the government. And from 1814 to 1842 no money was raised in this State by direct taxation except during the years in which the Erie and Champlain canals were in process of construction. To avoid a direct tax, however, it had been found necessary from time to time, to draw on the principal of the fund, and in 1834 it disappeared altogether and with it the bright dream of our forefathers of a commonwealth without taxation. Before the adoption of the Constitution of 1846 the fund had been succeeded by a general fund debt of $5,992,840.82. This was increased before the breaking out of the Civil War to a total of $6,505,684.37. This was the high-water mark of the general fund debt if we do not include in it the bounty debt of 1865. The Constitution of 1846 made provision for a sinking fund to meet this debt and its management and investment were intrusted to the Comptroller. In this way the last of the debt was paid in 1878.

Mr. Henry was removed from his office August 10, 1801, by reason of political changes in the Council of Appointment, and he then and there renounced politics forever. At the time of his death, in 1829, the leading Albany paper of the period spoke of Mr. Henry as "the idol of his friends; the ornament of his native city; the pride of the bar; the eloquent defender of the oppressed."

Henry's successor in office was Elisha Jenkins, a merchant and a Democrat (or Republican as the party was then called) of Hudson, who held the office from August 10, 1801, to March 26, 1806. Previous to his appointment as Comptroller he had served as Member of Assembly from Columbia county for the years 1795 to 1798. After his service as Comptroller he served three different periods as Secretary of State, to wit: From March 16, 1806, to February 16, 1807; from February 1, 1808, to February 1, 1810, and from February 1, 1811, to February 23, 1813. During his term as Comptroller there was a defalcation in the office of Treasurer, then held by Robert McClellan, and a more rigid system of testing the correctness of accounts was adopted, many features of which still survive. There was not much legislation affecting the office passed during the period of his incumbency; but the work of the office would seem to have been done in a systematic and business-like manner.

Mr. Jenkins was succeeded by Archibald McIntyre, a Democrat of the Clintonian order, of Albany, who, besides the reputation of a most excellent officer, has left behind him the record of a term of service in the office longer than that of any person who has filled it. He was appointed on March 26, 1806, and continued in office until February 12, 1821. He had previously served as Member of Assembly from Montgomery county for the years 1798, 1799, 1800, 1801, 1802 and 1804. The duties of the office had so far increased in 1811 as to render necessary the services of a deputy, and by chapter 78 his appointment was authorized, with substantially the same limitations which now exist. He cannot sign warrants so long as the Comptroller is within the State; nor can he act on the various boards. Comptroller McIntyre in 1817, under legislative authority, procured the aggregate valuation of the real estate in the several towns and wards of the State. By chapter 262 of the Laws of 1817 the Board of Commissioners of the Canal Fund was created, and the Comptroller made, *ex-officio*, a member of that board. This act contained a curious provision to the effect that a majority of the Commissioners, with the Comptroller, constitutes a quorum. No quorum of that board has ever been possible without the presence of the Comptroller.

This board, from that time to 1848, received and disbursed all canal moneys, audited the canal accounts, and in general transacted the financial business of the canal department. In 1848 the canal funds were turned over to the Treasurer and made subject to the warrant of the Canal Auditor. By his audit and warrant all accounts against the canals were paid; the management of the canal debt and sinking fund remaining, as before, in the Commissioners of the Canal Fund. In 1883 the duties devolving upon the Canal Auditor were transferred to the Comptroller's office. The majority of the Commissioners of the Canal Fund signed all checks on canal account prior to 1848. Since 1883, the Commissioners of the Canal Fund have had no duties to perform except to designate banks for the deposit of canal funds, and, ordinarily, to supervise the issuing of canal bonds.

The first canal debt bonds were issued in 1817 under legislative authority, and their disposition and the management of the sinking fund which was provided for their payment were put in the hands of the Commissioners of the Canal Fund. The amount of the debt that year was $200,000. As the canal system was extended, and later when the canals were enlarged, this debt was from time to time increased until in 1860 it reached the sum of $27,107,321.28. From that time it continuously decreased through the payments to, and the application of, the sinking fund, until on the 1st day of October, 1893, the last of this, the last bonded debt of the State, was paid. Something of financial history may be learned from a study of the rates of interest paid on these loans to the State. On the loan of 1817 the rate of interest was six per cent. From 1820 to 1830 the highest rate was six per cent and the lowest, five. From 1830 to 1840 a rate of five was sufficient. From 1840 to 1850 the rate advanced, the lowest being six and the highest seven per cent, the latter rate being in about 1842, the period of uncertainty as to the State's financial policy. From 1850 to 1860 the rate again fell to five and six per cent. In 1861 a small loan was made at seven. From 1870 to 1880 the rate was six per cent. This was the last of the old canal loan. By vote of the people in 1895 a loan of $9,000,000 was authorized to be used in the enlargement of the canals. The amounts thus far borrowed under that authority have been at the rate of three per cent.

6th COMPTROLLER

Perhaps the most notable circumstance of Comptroller McIntyre's term, and certainly one of the most notable in the whole history of the office, was his controversy with Daniel D. Tompkins. During the War of 1812 Governor Tompkins had been the agent both of the State and of the National Government, and in this dual capacity he had received and disbursed very large sums of money. For much of this money he had taken, or could produce, no vouchers, and, consequently, in 1819 he stood upon the Comptroller's books a debtor, if not a defaulter, to the State in the large amount of $120,000. He claimed, and his friends claimed for him, that he had honestly disbursed all the money that he had received, and that the apparent deficit was due to his acknowledged unbusiness-like methods, and in his failure to keep books of account, and to take vouchers. He was then Vice-President of the United States, and it was thought by the "Bucktail" Republicans that he was the only man who, in the State election of 1820, could beat Governor Clinton for re-election. This unsettled balance, which had been standing for several years on the books of the Comptroller, was a serious obstacle to the execution of their plan. Accordingly, the Legislature of 1819 passed an act requiring the Comptroller to settle the residue of the accounts of Governor Tompkins, and in the settlement to allow him the same premium on the amount of money borrowed by him "on his own responsibility" as was allowed others for like service; and further requiring the Comptroller to credit the Governor with sums paid by him, legally, to any person, and to call upon such persons to account for the money. Contrary, it was said, to what had been understood by those who had been instrumental in passing the act of 1819, Vice-President Tompkins, instead of presenting a claim for premium merely sufficient to offset the claim of the State against him, presented one for $250,000, and supported this claim by opinions both of experts and lawyers. This bill furnishes a commentary on the credit of the State in the perilous times of the War of 1812, or perhaps upon the value of the services of financial agents at that time. The brokerage charged by Governor Tompkins was at the rate of twenty-five per cent. The Comptroller, feeling that this was not the legislative intent, and ever watchful as he was of the State's interests, declined to allow the claim, on the ground that the Governor had not borrowed the money "on his own responsibility," but on the joint responsibility of the State and himself. The Comptroller offered to submit the soundness of his position to the Judges of the Supreme Court, and to join with the Judges, if it was desired, the Chancellor or the Attorney-General. But this Mr. Tompkins declined on the ground that all of these proposed referees were politically hostile to him. Correspondence relating to the matter, and marked by great bitterness of tone, took place between these eminent officials; and in this the Comptroller showed not only a familiarity with accounts, but a facility with the pen, which was a surprise to those who had not known him intimately. This matter occupied much of the attention of the Legislature for two years, and gave rise to protracted and animated debates, and there is no doubt that it entered largely into the defeat of Governor Tompkins by Clinton in 1820. The controversy was finally settled under an act of the Legislature of 1820, which directed the Comptroller to balance the accounts upon the filing of a release from Governor Tompkins of all his claims against the State. It had required no small amount of courage for Comptroller McIntyre to engage in a trial of strength with this idol of the State. Daniel D. Tompkins was four times elected Governor of the State, and twice elected Vice-President. He was a man of great personal magnetism; with large abilities, and he held a place in the affections of the people of this State which has scarcely been equaled by any of our citizens since his time.

At no time in the history of the State has the Comptroller's office been more ably filled, and occupied a more prominent position, than during the administration of Archibald McIntyre. He had the unbounded confidence of all, and although there were several Councils of Appointment during his term of service which were hostile to him, no one seems to have thought of removing him. He was regarded as a public servant whose services could not well be spared to the State. He was held in a measure responsible for the defeat of Governor Tompkins, and, although Clinton was elected, the Legislature and the Council of Appointment were decidedly hostile both to Clinton and to him, and on February 12, 1821, Mr. McIntyre was removed, and John Savage appointed in his place. His removal would have created far greater dissatisfaction than it did, although the dissatisfaction was considerable, had not his successor been a man of concededly great ability. Mr. McIntyre was, the year of his removal, nominated as the Clintonian candidate for Senator from the middle district, and, although strenuous efforts were made to defeat him, he was elected by a substantial majority.

In 1822 he was, with John B. Yates, appointed agent for the State lotteries. The Constitution of 1821 had forbidden any further lotteries within the State, and authorized the Legislature to pass laws preventing the sale of tickets except in the lotteries already established by law. These were mostly instituted under the law of 1814 for the purpose of aiding literary institutions. By the act appointing him, the agents were invested with sole authority to issue and sell all lottery tickets which, for the future, were to be issued to pay some hundreds of thousands of dollars due various institutions. The legislative intent was carried out by the agents to the satisfaction of the beneficiaries, and also with satisfactory pecuniary results to the agents themselves. Upon his retirement from his agency Mr. McIntyre was able to withdraw both from politics and business.

One would hardly expect to find in the books of account in the Comptroller's office anything in the nature of a history of morals, but the receipts from various lotteries forms a no inconsiderable part of the receipts of the State for a number of years. This opens up a view which almost shocks modern sensibility. Lotteries were not only authorized by the State, but they were in the main devoted to beneficent purposes. Union College owes no inconsiderable part of her early usefulness to money derived from State lotteries. Indeed, the institution of State lotteries in New York may almost be attributed to the efforts of that truly great and good man, the Rev. Dr. Eliphalet Nott. The first moneys ever appropriated by New York for the purposes of free schools were raised by lottery.

John Savage, of Salem, a lawyer, and a Democrat of the "Bucktail" stamp, was the fifth Comptroller, and at the time of his appointment he was not new to public life. He had been district attorney of the fourth district from 1806 to 1811, and again from 1812 to 1813; Member of Assembly from Washington county in 1814, and Member of the Fourteenth and Fifteenth Congresses. He rounded out his official career with eight years (from 1823 to 1831) of honored service as Chief Justice of the Supreme Court. As a public official it has been said that "he exhibited candor, industry, caution and excellent judgment." No higher qualities can be given to any official. Later in life the positions of Chancellor and Treasurer of the United States were offered to him but declined. During his term of office there was no substantial change or enlargement of the powers and duties of the office, aside from the power given to invest money belonging to the common school fund. The common school fund had its origin in 1805, and was, as the determination for free schools became more manifest, an application to a school system of the Utopian vision of the makers of the State, who sought to pay all the expenses of maintaining the government by interest from its invested funds. The common school fund has, unlike the general fund, steadily increased. By the act of 1805 the proceeds of the first 500,000 acres of vacant and unappropriated land sold by the Surveyor-General were appropriated as a permanent fund for the support of common schools. Other sources of revenue were from time to time turned into this fund, until from its small beginning of $58,757.24 in 1805, it has now productive investments aggregating $4,448,140.77. It is a noteworthy fact that no direct tax for school purposes was laid by the State until 1853, the interest of the fund alone being appropriated. How small a portion the income plays in maintaining the schools of the State today can be seen in the fact that the State for the year 1896 appropriated for educational purposes $4,970,134.53, and this is not a quarter of the amount expended in the State for the purpose of free schools, when the local contributions are taken into account. Judge Savage was the last Comptroller who owed his selection to the Council of Appointment.

The Constitutional Convention of 1821, in deference to strong public demand, had abolished that disgraceful anomaly, and by section 6 of article 4 had provided that "the Secretary of State, Comptroller, Treasurer, Attorney-General, Surveyor-General and Commissioner-General shall be appointed as follows: The Senate and Assembly shall each openly nominate one person for the said offices respectively; after which they shall meet again, and if they shall agree in their nominations the person so nominated shall be appointed to the office for which he shall be nominated. If they shall disagree, the appointment shall be made by the joint ballot of the Senators and Members of Assembly. The Secretary of State, Comptroller, Treasurer, Attorney-General, Surveyor-General and Commissioner-General shall hold their office for three years, unless sooner removed by concurrent resolution of the Senate and Assembly."

10th COMPTROLLER

The Legislature, on the 13th day of February, 1823, elected, in the manner provided by law, William L. Marcy, a lawyer and a Democrat, of Albany, to succeed Savage. There was a contest in the caucus over his nomination, his opponent being Genl. James Tallmadge, a man of conspicuous ability and influence in the Senate. The power of Mr. Van Buren, however, turned the scale in Mr. Marcy's favor. The only public position which he had previously held was Adjutant-General, but from that time on his name is closely linked with the history of the State and Union. He was Comptroller for six years, Judge of the Supreme Court for two years, and United States Senator for two years. He was three times elected Governor, and defeated in his fourth run for that office by William H. Seward. He was appointed Secretary of War by President Polk in 1845, and Secretary of State by President Pierce in 1853. He had for years, under Mr. Van Buren, been a leader of that most influential political body which has become known to history as the

"Albany Regency." The remaining members are understood to have been at that time Silas Wright, Azariah C. Flagg, Edwin Croswell, John A. Dix, James Porter and Benjamin Knower. The records of the State show that these men, while building up a compact and powerful political organization, did not neglect their own personal and political advancement.

One of the vouchers in the Comptroller's office played a prominent part in the last of Mr. Marcy's gubernatorial campaigns—a circumstance which, Thurlow Weed says, Mr. Marcy pronounced the most disagreeable of his entire public career. While serving as Supreme Court Judge, and on Circuit in Niagara county, he included in his bill of expenses an item as follows: "For mending my pantaloons, 50c." In the Seward campaign Thurlow Weed, then the editor of the Albany *Evening Journal*, learned of this fact and published the story. It was taken up by the press generally throughout the State, and Mr. Marcy, with all his fine organization and numberless friends, found himself for the time being, like Spain's chivalry, "laughed away."

11th COMPTROLLER

The item, however, exhibits the scrupulous exactness of the man. Instead of presenting the bill with an indefinite amount of incidentals, he itemized it thus particularly to his own disadvantage; but, as Mr. Weed afterward admitted, it was a credit to his honesty.

It was during Mr. Marcy's term that much of the work on the Erie canal was done, and the careful scrutiny which the bills for this work received was largely instrumental in keeping the cost within the estimates. He took ground as chief financial officer of the State against the construction of the Chenango and Genesee Valley canals, for the reason that these canals would not, in his judgment, pay the expenses of maintenance and the interest on the debt which would be incurred in their construction. While friends of the measures endeavored to convince the Legislature that the Comptroller was wrong in his calculation, the result, when these works were finally completed, fully justified the Comptroller's view. As Governor he made some friends, and more enemies, by adhering to the same careful course he had maintained as Comptroller. In 1826 the Legislature created the Canal Board, and the Comptroller was made *ex-officio* a member of it, and he has continued to act as such member down to the present.

On the 27th day of January, 1829, the Legislature elected as the successor of Mr. Marcy a man who, in his time, made a great impression upon State and National politics—Silas Wright, of Canton, a lawyer and a Regency Democrat. He had previously been Surrogate of St. Lawrence county, State Senator from the fourth district for the years 1824, 1825, 1826 and 1827, and a Member of the Twentieth and Twenty-first Congresses. In the latter position he had achieved considerable reputation. After his five years' service as Comptroller he held with high honor, for nearly twelve years, the position of United States Senator. During the term of Mr. Van Buren as President he was considered to voice the administration in his public utterances. He served faithfully and intelligently upon some of the most important committees. He resigned to take the office of Governor, which office he held in 1845 and 1846, and was defeated for re-election by John Young in November, 1846. Mr. Wright continued the careful and conservative policy of his predecessor as to expenditures. He took strong ground against the numerous and extensive raids on the treasury which were then organized. His reports were always plain, business-like papers, which set out in intelligible language the consequences of the rapidly-increasing expenses. Mr. Wright in many ways was a remarkable man. The public positions which he held were varied, and it was a great test of his adaptability to be able to fill the duties of these various positions with much more than ordinary success. In 1831 the financial law of the State was revised, and the provisions relating to the powers and duties of the Comptroller were codified and arranged.

Upon his election as United States Senator Mr. Wright resigned and was succeeded by Azariah C. Flagg, of Plattsburgh, a lawyer and a Regency Democrat, who was elected on January 11, 1834. He had been a Member of Assembly from Clinton county in 1823 and 1824, and held the office of Secretary of State from 1826 to 1833. He had run counter to public opinion in 1823 as the leader of the Assembly opposition to the Electoral law—a law designed to give to the people directly the power of chosing the presidential electors, instead of leaving that power vested in the Legislature, as had been the law theretofore. The Albany Regency had determined to prevent any change, and succeeded in warding off legislative action. The measure, however, met the cordial approval of the people, and that fact, together with the removal of Governor Clinton as Canal Commissioner—a position in which his uncompensated services had been of the greatest value—swept Clinton, whose political fortunes then seemed at their lowest ebb, triumphantly into the gubernatorial chair. But it was a principle of the Albany Regency, and of Martin Van Buren, then at its head, never to forget a man who had fallen or suffered in their service; and it was in reward for Mr. Flagg's unpopular opposition to the Electoral bill that in 1826 he was chosen Secretary of State. Mr. Flagg has the distinction of having served longer as Comptroller than any other incumbent of the office, with the exception of Archibald McIntyre. He held the office from January 11, 1834, to February 4, 1839, and again from February 7, 1842, to November 7, 1847. During his first term he was a member of the commission for the erection of the State Hall, and that building still stands as a monument to the Commission's good judgment in architecture, and in the adaptation of means to an end. Upon the completion of the State Hall the old State Hall, corner of Lodge and State streets, was sold by the Commission. By chapters 2 and 150 of the Laws of 1837 the Comptroller was made the custodian of moneys received from the United States, since known as the United States Deposit Fund. Theoretically this money was not given to the several States, but was to be subject to repayment whenever called for. The National Government will hardly, at this late day, call for these moneys. If it did not feel compelled to do so in the trying financial straits of the war it is not likely that it will do so in times of peace. But these moneys have always been kept as a separate fund, substantially as required by the act of 1837, and the principal, through all changes of, and losses from, investment, has been kept intact.

By chapter 260 of the Laws of 1838 the Comptroller, to guard against counterfeiting, was authorized and required to have engraved and printed in the best manner, circulating notes to be issued to the incorporated banks of the State, and to countersign the same; and a system was inaugurated for the deposit of securities in the Comptroller's office which should be a guaranty for the notes issued by the banks—a system very similar to that later adopted by the United States for National banks. One feature which would be regarded as a most unwise one today formed a part of this plan; the banks were authorized to deposit one-half the security in bonds and mortgages. The bill also provided that banking associations should file with the Comptroller a semi-annual report of the transactions of the bank. This was practically the inauguration of the supervision of the banks, which was later transferred to the Banking Department. The Legislature had, in 1829, at the time of the creation of the safety fund, authorized the appointment of three Bank Commissioners, whose duty it was to visit the banks, examine their condition, and report to the Legislature. The office of Bank Commissioner was abolished in 1843, and the power of supervision possessed by them was then transferred to the Comptroller, and he continued to retain that power until 1851, when the Banking Department was created. It was during Mr. Flagg's first term that the great financial panic of 1837 took place, and the State's financial condition at that time was not all that might be desired. There was a large debt, mostly incurred in the construction of canals. The revenues had very much decreased, and a new way of raising funds must be used to meet the liabilities of the State and maintain her credit. Matters financial in the State went from bad to worse. In 1842, after long debate, the Legislature passed an act authorizing the laying of a tax of one mill upon every dollar of real and personal property in the State, and pledging the revenues of the State for the payment of its liabilities, and suspending all public work, except where great loss would come to the State by such suspension. In this manner the credit of the State was made secure and its obligations met. This act was prepared and advocated by Mr. Flagg. The significance of this legislation is found largely in the fact that from 1826 to 1842 no State tax for general purposes had been required.

The long lease of power which the Democrats had held in this State was broken in the fall of 1838 by the combined efforts of the Whigs and Anti-Masons, and, accordingly, on the 4th of January, 1839, Mr. Flagg was removed, and Bates Cook, of Lewiston, a lawyer and an Anti-Mason was chosen by the Legislature in his place. Mr. Cook's only previous official service of note had been as Member of the Twenty-second Congress. His appointment was largely due to the influence and representations of William H. Seward, then the Governor, and Thurlow Weed. He had been associated with these gentlemen in the prosecution of the abductors of William Morgan, and, like Mr. Seward and Mr. Fillmore, received his political start from Anti-Masonic influence. Mr. Cook soon had an opportunity to show Mr. Weed his appreciation of the favor done him. Chapter 1 of the Laws of 1840 authorized the Comptroller and Secretary of State to enter into a contract with Thurlow Weed to do the printing for the Legislature, executive offices and various boards, at prices not exceeding ordinary prices in Albany.

This seems to have been the first time these officers were intrusted with this responsibility, and it was not until 1846 that the general power was definitely conferred upon them. Subsequent legislation has added to the printing board then created the Attorney-General, so far as legislative printing is concerned; but as to department printing, the Secretary of State and the Comptroller are still clothed with the authority of letting the contract.

By chapter 295 of the Laws of 1840 the Comptroller was assigned quarters in the State Hall, together with the other State officers, and that building was made the headquarters of the Canal Board, and there both still remain, although the Comptroller, from time to time, as the needs have compelled, has taken to himself more rooms, so that his offices now occupy the entire first floor of the building.

On January 27, 1841, the Legislature elected John A. Collier, of Binghamton, a leading lawyer and an Anti-Mason, to succeed Bates Cook. He had previously served as District Attorney of Broome county from June 11, 1818, to February 22, 1822, and had served his district in the Twenty-second Congress. After his retirement from the office of Comptroller he was appointed, with Chancellor Walworth, to codify the laws, but declined to serve. This was a high tribute to his ability.

During 1841 the Comptroller's office was examined by a legislative committee, to ascertain if warrants had been drawn in conformity with the law, and the funds properly disbursed. The office was found able to stand the fire of a rigid investigation.

Mr. Collier had been a Federalist and a Clintonian, but it was as an Anti-Mason that he was elected both to Congress and as Comptroller. He, too, was largely indebted for his appointment as Comptroller to the potent influence of Thurlow Weed. The administration was a short but efficient one, and Mr. Collier proved himself through life an able and discreet man.

The Legislature, which for several years had been Whig, in 1842 became Democratic, so that by concurrent resolution, on February seventh they were enabled to remove John A. Collier and re-appoint Azariah C. Flagg. During his second term Mr. Flagg performed the multiplying duties of the office with his usual fidelity, and to the satisfaction of the people of the State. There seems to have been no important enlargement of the duties of the office during this period. By various statutes, passed prior to the Constitution of 1846, the State had loaned its credit to a number of corporations, mostly railroad, until, in 1845, the State debt thus incurred, called the "contingent debt," amounted to $5,235,700. Provision was made for a sinking fund, and the management of this fund was placed with the Comptroller. Corporations have no souls, and, consequently, we find that of the credit thus loaned the State lost $3,665,700. From the additions to and accumulations of the sinking fund, the last of the contingent debt was extinguished in 1877.

By chapter 350 of the Laws of 1847, passed during his term, the Comptroller was required to make a report of the fiscal year before the close of the calendar year, and to present the same to the Legislature shortly after the commencement of its session.

But at this point a new method of chosing a Comptroller was introduced in the organic law. Section 1 of article 5 of the Constitution of 1846 provides that "The Secretary of State, Comptroller, Treasurer and Attorney-General shall be chosen at a general election, and shall hold their offices for two years." The constitutional provision was supplemented by chapter 240 of the Laws of 1846. The first man elected by the people to the office was Millard Fillmore, of Buffalo, an able lawyer and a Whig. He had been a Member of Assembly from Buffalo in 1829, 1830 and 1831, and a Member from his district to the Twenty-third, Twenty-fifth, Twenty-sixth and Twenty-seventh Congresses. During his term as Comptroller he was nominated and elected Vice-President on the ticket with Zachary Taylor, and upon the latter's death, on July 9, 1850, he succeeded to the Presidency. As President he is, perhaps, more distinguished as the signer of the "Fugitive Slave Law" than for any other one thing. He was elected Comptroller and Vice-President as a Whig, but by the signing of that obnoxious measure he alienated very many of his old Whig associates. He was, however, a clean, able man. In politics he was thought by many to have been a favorite of fortune. Some one of his acquaintances is said to have remarked, at the time of his election as Vice-President, that he felt sorry for General Taylor, because the General never could live out his term against Fillmore's luck. Mr. Fillmore resigned the office of Comptroller on the 17th of February, 1849, to assume the duties of Vice-President.

The Legislature appointed Washington Hunt, a lawyer of prominence and a Whig, of Lockport, to succeed him. Mr. Hunt had been County Judge of Niagara county from 1836 to 1841, and had been a member of the Twenty-eighth, Twenty-ninth and Thirtieth Congresses. He was nominated and elected Comptroller in the fall of 1849. In 1850 he was elected Governor over Horatio Seymour, but in 1852 he was in turn defeated in his run for the second term by Seymour. He made an excellent record as Governor during the years 1851 and 1852. It was upon Mr. Hunt's recommendation that the duties of supervising and superintending the banking business of the State was transferred to the Banking Department, specially created for the purpose. He felt that a greater burden of responsibility was being imposed upon the office of Comptroller than could be satisfactorily sustained. This is one of the rare illustrations of a desire to surrender power. But what relief was gained by the transfer of the supervision of the banks was replaced by the duty which was imposed of superintending the business of insurance in this State.

All insurance companies, prior to 1846, had been incorporated by special acts, but the Constitution of that year prohibited the creation of such corporations, except under general laws. In 1849 the Legislature passed a general law for the incorporation of insurance companies. By the terms of the act the duty of organizing and regulating insurance companies in this State, both domestic and foreign, was conferred upon the Comptroller. This was the first State supervision of insurance. The duty remained with the Comptroller until January 1, 1860, when the act creating the Department of Insurance went into effect.

The Comptroller's office feels proud of its two healthy and useful children—the Banking Department and the Insurance Department, which have been efficiently serving the State and protecting the interests of its citizens for many years, and it ventures to believe that the early tuition that they received from the parent department helped to form their habits and prepare them for their career.

Mr. Hunt resigned the Comptrollership December 18, 1850, two weeks before he was to enter upon his duties as Governor, and Philo C. Fuller, a Whig, of Geneseo, was appointed in his place. Mr. Fuller had, in early life, been a clerk in the land office of Mr. James Wadsworth. Thurlow Weed met him at that time and recognized in him abilities of a high order. It was probably at Mr. Weed's suggestion that he first entered public life; it was certainly upon Mr. Weed's recommendation that he was appointed Comptroller. It was one of the great secrets of Thurlow Weed's long retention of political power that whenever he saw capability he sought, and, to use a ranchman's expression, "corralled it." Mr. Fuller was Member of Assembly from Livingston county in 1829 and 1830, State Senator in 1831 and 1832, and Member of the Twenty-third and Twenty-fourth Congresses. Later he moved to Michigan, and, being elected to the Legislature, he was chosen Speaker. He was appointed Assistant Postmaster-General in the Harrison administration, but, being unwilling to follow President Tyler into the Democratic camp, he resigned, and returned to New York. He performed the duties of his office of Comptroller with ability, although doubt of his capacity was felt at the time of his appointment.

For the forty years from 1840 to 1880 the Comptroller's office was one of difficulty. During the first half of that period there was seldom a year when the expenditures did not exceed the appropriations, and when the Comptroller was not obliged to report a deficit at the end of the year. There was also during that same period a rapidly-increasing canal debt, and the Comptroller was in duty bound to find a market for bonds and the means to meet the interest when it became due. In the latter half of this period it was the Comptroller's duty to see that the means were at hand to pay the principal of this and other bonded debts, and the increased expenditures caused by the war.

Mr. Fuller was succeeded January 1, 1852, by John C. Wright, a Democrat and lawyer, of Schenectady. He had been County Judge of Schoharie county from 1833 to 1838, and State Senator from the third district in 1843, 1844, 1845 and 1846. He was an opponent of the Albany Regency during his senatorial career. He was a ready debater but of impulsive temper, and at one time engaged in a personal rencounter with Colonel Young on the floor of the Senate chamber. His administration was unmarked by any peculiar enlargement of the official power, or by distinguished executive ability. That things run so smoothly that no attention is attracted is oftentimes strong evidence of a successful working machinery. By an act of the Legislature of 1851 the Comptroller was authorized to borrow three millions per year for three years for the completion of the canal enlargement.

Mr. Wright served one term, and was succeeded, January 1, 1854, by James M. Cook, a lawyer and a Whig, of Ballston. Mr. Cook was a member of the Constitutional Convention of 1846, Senator from the thirteenth district for 1848, 1849, 1850 and 1851, and from the fifteenth district in 1864 and 1865. He served as State Treasurer during the years 1852 and 1853, and was Bank Superintendent from January 30, 1856, to January 11, 1861. He was thus continuously in the service of the State from 1848 to 1861, a period of thirteen years. In 1854 the Comptroller was authorized to appoint three commissioners to investigate the State prisons and report on their financial condition, and also upon such laws as they deemed proper for their better regulation. Under this abuses were corrected, and the Comptroller was given closer supervision of the prisons.

For a short time in 1858 the Whig leaders had under favorable consideration the nomination of Mr. Cook for Governor, but circumstances forced a change, and E. D. Morgan was nominated and elected.

On January 1, 1856, Lorenzo Burrows, a banker and an "American" or "Know Nothing," of Albion, became Comptroller. He had been a member of the Thirty-first and Thirty-second Congresses. He later served as Regent of the University by appointment made February 17, 1858, and in November, 1858, was one of the candidates of the "American party" for Governor against E. D. Morgan. To the time of his death, many years afterward, he never failed to make at least one visit yearly to the Comptroller's office, and always maintained a lively interest in its affairs.

After one term of service Mr. Burrows was succeeded by Sanford E. Church, a lawyer and a Democrat, also of Albion. Mr. Church had been a Member of Assembly from Orleans county in 1842; District Attorney of the same county from 1846 to 1850; Lieutenant-Governor from 1850 to 1854. He ran for re-election as Comptroller in 1859 and was defeated, and again in 1863 and was also defeated. He was elected one of the Delegates-at-Large to the Constitutional Convention in 1867, and was Chief Judge of the Court of Appeals from May, 1870, to May 20, 1880, when he died. In all these various positions Mr. Church showed a broad, liberal spirit, and great mental force. His reports as Comptroller are valuable State papers, expressed in clear, strong and forcible language. It is sufficient to say of Judge Church, that, as Comptroller, he brought the same care, attention and strong mental grasp to his duties that afterward won for him eminence and fame as Chief Judge of our highest court.

Robert Denniston, a gentleman farmer and Republican, of Salisbury's Mills, became Comptroller January 1, 1860, having been elected at the November election of 1859 over Sanford E. Church. He had been Assemblyman from Orange county in 1845, and Senator from the second district in 1841, 1842, 1843, 1844, 1845, 1846 and 1847, and had been an unsuccessful candidate against Mr. Church for the office of Comptroller in November, 1857. He was thus Comptroller in the first year of the war, at the inauguration of high taxes and the large expenditures of that period. His administration was wise and conservative.

On January 1, 1862, Lucius Robinson, an able lawyer of Elmira, assumed the duties of the office. Mr. Robinson was a Democrat, but at the breaking out of the war he was strongly for the Union cause, and it was on the Union ticket that he was elected Comptroller, and he was re-elected on the same ticket in 1863. At the close of the war, he resumed his place in the Democratic party, from which he had never been fully estranged. He ran as a Democrat against Thomas Hillhouse, in 1865, and was beaten. He had been District Attorney of Greene county from 1837 to 1839, and Member of Assembly from Chemung county in 1860 and 1861. He was re-elected Comptroller in November, 1863, and again in November, 1875. He was a member of the Constitutional Commission of 1872, Governor of this State for the years 1877, 1878 and 1879, and defeated for re-election in November, 1879, by Alonzo B. Cornell. He was Comptroller during the dark days of our Civil War. At no period, however, of its history was the work of the office more carefully managed. For the six years from 1860 to 1866, the canal and general fund debts were reduced $8,000,000. In the four years of the war, the State expenditures for arms, bounties, clothing, equipments and various military purposes were upwards of $20,000,000. To meet these large and abnormal expenses, required of the Comptroller resourceful ability. When specie was at a high premium in 1863 and 1864, Mr. Robinson earnestly recommended the payment of the State's bonded debt, both principal and interest, in specie. The Legislature, however, disregarded the recommendation. There was precedent in the office for such a course. Comptroller Flagg, upon the suspension of specie payment in 1837, made good the difference between the depreciated currency and coin. Comptroller Allen followed the lead of Mr. Robinson, and urged the payment of these debts in coin. This was not done, however, until 1870, when the State went into the open market and bought coin to pay the interest on its bonds, and continued this policy until the resumption of specie payment in 1879. This course, however, was not pursued with reference to the bounty debt. In 1865, against the advice and almost protest of the Comptroller, the Legislature assumed the bounty debt of the various counties of the State, and for that purpose it became necessary for the State to issue its bonds to the amount of $27,644,000. The act authorizing the creation of the debt provided for a sinking fund, and the managing of this fund and the issuing of the bonds was given to the Comptroller. This debt was extinguished year by year until it disappeared from the Comptroller's books in 1877. It was during Mr. Robinson's term, in 1863, that $66,000 were appropriated to purchase the lands adjoining the then Capitol, and bounded by State, Hawk and Congress streets. This was probably the first money expended on "That lofty pile where senates dictate laws."

In 1862, the Legislature placed an item in the appropriation bill which still remains law. It provides that the Comptroller shall not draw his warrant, except for salaries and regular expenses, until the person entitled to the money shall present a detailed account, verified by affidavit as to services; and if for traveling expenses, a detailed account specifying the distance and places from and to which, and receipted vouchers for all disbursements. By chapter 419 of the Laws of 1864, the officers of all hospitals, orphan asylums, benevolent associations, educational and charitable institutions were required to report to the Comptroller their financial condition, with their receipts and disbursements. The Comptroller was, by concurrent resolution of the Legislature, the same year appointed, with the Governor and the Secretary of State, to take action properly to receive the returning veterans, and for the health of the recruits. Mr. Robinson was a man of great executive force, strict honesty, and with the courage of his convictions.

He was succeeded by Thomas Hillhouse on the 1st of January, 1866, Mr. Hillhouse having been elected in November, 1865. He was a gentleman farmer and a Republican from Geneva, and had been Senator from the twenty-sixth district in 1860 and 1861, and Adjutant-General of the State from August 19, 1861, to January 1, 1863. He still survives as the honored president of the Metropolitan Trust Company, of New York. Thurlow Weed in his autobiography says: "For my direct responsibility in the selection of Bates Cook, John A. Collier, Millard Fillmore, Washington Hunt, Philo C. Fuller, James M. Cook, Robert Denniston and Thomas Hillhouse, I look back with pardonable pride, for in few ways could better service have been rendered to the State and people." Mr. Hillhouse certainly deserved the confidence reposed in him. He was careful, conservative and able.

On January 1, 1868, Mr. Hillhouse gave way to William F. Allen, a distinguished lawyer and a Democrat, of Oswego. Mr. Allen served as Member of Assembly from Oswego in 1843 and 1844, and was appointed United States District Attorney in 1845, and was appointed Judge of the Supreme Court in the fifth district in 1847, and elected to the same position in the fall election of 1855. He was re-elected Comptroller in November, 1869, but resigned June 14, 1870, to accept an appointment as Judge of the Court of Appeals. This latter place he held with great distinction until his death, in June, 1878. In 1864 he was the slated Democratic candidate for Governor. Horatio Seymour was then Governor, and Mr. Allen's friends at least understood that Mr. Seymour wished a renomination as a compliment, but would decline. To their consternation, however, Mr. Seymour came before the convention, thanked its members for the honor done him, and accepted. It was during Mr. Allen's administration that the Comptroller was authorized to appoint an agent to examine into the reports submitted to him by the various charitable institutions. By chapter 281 of the Laws of 1870, the Comptroller was made, *ex-officio*, a member of the State Commission of Public Charities. Judge Allen was distinguished by talents of the highest order, and his long public career was a useful one to the State.

It is an interesting political fact that in the campaign of 1869 Judge Allen had as his opponent in the run for Comptroller Horace Greeley. Mr. Greeley's election was earnestly opposed by many of the leading Republicans of the State. A letter of Thurlow Weed was made public, in which he appealed very strongly to the people of the State to vote against Mr. Greeley. He based his opposition quite largely upon the fact that Mr. Greeley's time would have to be divided between his editorial duties in New York and the Comptroller's office in Albany. He then went on to say: "The office of Comptroller is most laborious and responsible. I have known its incumbents for considerably more than half a century. Among them were Archibald McIntyre, John Savage, William L. Marcy, Silas Wright, Jr., Azariah C. Flagg, John A. Collier, Washington Hunt, Philo A. Fuller, James M. Cook, Thos. Hillhouse and others, distinguished for ability and industry, not one of whom have attempted to attend to any other business, and all of whom found constant and full occupation, physical and mental, in the discharge of their public duties. Without regard to other reasons for withholding my vote from Mr. Greeley, I consider those which I have stated sufficient. In his opponent, William F. Allen, I found a capable and enlightened man, with some experience, much industry and peculiar fitness for the duties of the office. I have known him first, as an able and useful member of our Legislature, and next as an eminently upright judge."

Upon the resignation of Judge Allen, Asher P. Nichols, a lawyer and Democrat, of Buffalo, was appointed, and, in the fall of the same year, 1870, he was elected to fill the unexpired term. He had been previously a State Senator from the thirty-first district in 1868 and 1869. He ran for the office of Comptroller in 1871 and again in 1873, and was defeated both times by Nelson K. Hopkins. Mr. Nichols was a man of ability, who commanded the highest respect of those who knew him. He was distinguished somewhat for an old-time formal courtesy of manner. It is fair to Mr. Nichols to say that the deficiency in the treasury which Mr. Hopkins found upon his advent was not due to him, or to lack of recommendations on his part, but rather to the attempt of the Tweed *regime* in the Legislature to make a tax rate that would continue them in power. "Among the faithless, faithful only he."

Mr. Hopkins was a lawyer and a Republican from Buffalo, and he entered upon the discharge of the duties of the office on January 1, 1872, and continued therein for four years. This was the beginning and the end of his career in State politics, but in those four years he left a record of splendid and faithful work.

He found upon his entry into office that there had been for several years a growing deficiency in the general fund. In 1869 the excess of appropriations over receipts was $1,493,181.28; in 1870, $2,355,927.40; in 1871, $2,748,595.56; in 1872, $1,785,762.97; in 1873, $254,253.53; making for the five years an aggregate deficiency of $8,637,720.74.

The money to the extent of this deficiency had been supplied to the treasury by using the moneys from the bounty debt sinking fund. Heroic treatment was necessary, so disregarding political effect Mr. Hopkins advocated and secured the adoption of the highest tax rate in the history of the State, to wit, nine and three-eighths mills on the dollar, and three and one-half mills of this amount went to make up the deficiency. In this way the bounty debt sinking fund was again made good. In 1873 the Comptroller was given power to examine into the affairs of the prisons, with the power of a court of record to subpœna witnesses, etc., and the same year he was authorized in person, or by agent, to visit the various State institutions and examine their books, papers and vouchers, both of which powers are still inherent in the Comptroller's office. The same year he was authorized to set aside cancellations of tax titles made by him whenever it appeared that fraud, misrepresentation or the suppression of a fact, or a mistake of fact, had induced the cancellation. This power, with slight modification, still remains.

During Mr. Hopkins' four years of service the bounty debt was reduced $14,401,700, and he was able to congratulate the Legislature and the people of the State at the close of his term on the prospect of a substantial reduction of tax.

On the 1st of January, 1876, Lucius Robinson again assumed the office of Comptroller, which he held one year. He had defeated in the election the November preceding Francis E. Spinner, whose services and signature are so well known as to make comment unnecessary. His second administration of the office was distinguished by the same care-taking ability which was manifest in the first. The reduction of the bounty debt and other indebtedness of the State continued. He was elected Governor in 1876.

The first official act of Governor Robinson was the appointment of Frederic P. Olcott, of Albany, as Comptroller. It is a matter of secret political history that Governor Tilden had desired to appoint Daniel Magone to the office, and that for that reason Mr. Robinson would not resign until it was too late for Governor Tilden to act. But he had to act promptly, because, if no appointment were made before the Legislature convened, the power to fill the vacancy would then be in that body. Governor Robinson improved the fleeting moment. Mr. Olcott, as the head of the firm of F. P. Olcott & Co., had been the State's agent in transactions relating to the bounty debt, and, to Mr. Robinson's mind, he had exhibited abilities which would make of him a valuable Comptroller. That the Governor was not mistaken, Mr. Olcott's career, both as Comptroller, and since his retirement from that office, as president of the Central Trust Company, abundantly proves. He served out Mr. Robinson's unexpired term, and was elected in November, 1877, over C. V. R. Ludington, but was defeated for re-election in 1879 by James W. Wadsworth. This was the only political office which he ever held. Early in his term his attention was attracted to the abnormal quantities of soft soap which one of the small State charitable institutions was using, and he became satisfied that "soft soap," like Pickwick's "warming pan," was a cover for something hidden. Among the vouchers for May and June, 1875, were vouchers for seventy-eight barrels of soft soap at a cost of $350, which, at the same rate, would make an aggregate of $2,100 per year. The aggregate expenditure for soft soap for the institution during the six years ending June 30, 1876, had been $3,963.60. An investigation was instituted at the Comptroller's request by the State Board of Charities, and it was found that "soft soap" in that instance meant the laying out of roads and beautifying grounds to an extent that the Comptroller's office would not have paid. The designing institution learned to its surprise that the Comptroller could not stand too much "soft soap." These revelations led the Comptroller to ask the Legislature for power to investigate thoroughly all the charitable institutions. This work was ably done by Edgar K. Apgar, who made an admirable report, and this report was the means of establishing a more thorough and systematic supervision of these institutions by the Comptroller's department. In his report, transmitted to the Legislature on the 1st of January, 1878, Mr. Olcott said: "Each of these institutions is now separate and distinct from its fellows, and each is governed by a local board of trustees. It is evident, therefore, that there is no general system governing all, but each is a law unto itself. There is no department of government which exercises any supervision over their affairs or that has more than a superficial knowledge of the manner in which they are conducted. * * * I would recommend for your consideration the policy of abolishing all local boards of trustees and the erection of a system by which the different institutions shall be managed by one controlling power. As it is, the responsibility for losses and expensive management is not centred in any one."

24th COMPTROLLER

On the 2d of May, 1878 (the good faith of Olcott's work in handling the bounty bonds having been called in question), he sent a communication to the Legislature which more than proved the faithful and able manner in which he had performed his duties in respect to these bonds. The report was called out by a resolution of the Senate. Some strongly partisan members believed that they could unearth thereby, if not crookedness, at least large compensation for services performed. The attempt failed signally. Mr. Olcott's administration of the office ranks with the ablest.

James W. Wadsworth, a gentleman farmer and Republican, from Geneseo, became Comptroller January, 1, 1880, and was one of the youngest men who have held the office. He had as a boy served with his father, the gallant and lamented General James S. Wadsworth in the Civil War. He was Member of Assembly from Livingston county in 1878 and 1879, and was distinguished in the latter year as the only Republican in the Legislature who would not vote for the return of Roscoe Conkling to the United States Senate, and that, too, notwithstanding the fact that Mr. Conkling had been duly nominated by a Republican caucus. Mr. Conkling and he afterwards forgot differences and became quite warmly attached. He ran again for Comptroller in 1885 but was defeated. He has faithfully represented a discriminating constituency in the Forty-seventh, Forty-eighth, Fifty-second, Fifty-third and Fifty-fourth Congresses, and has been re-elected to the Fifty-fifth. Mr. Wadsworth took great interest in the affairs of the office during his term, and his sterling integrity and good judgment made him a most excellent officer. In 1880, by chapter 100, the Comptroller was authorized to issue bonds in anticipation of the State tax, payable on or before the fifteenth day of May following, such bonds not to exceed in amount one-half of such tax. It was necessary for Mr. Wadsworth to inaugurate the system of collecting taxes on corporations. The original bill for that purpose was passed in 1880. It has been amended from time to time, but the whole duty of enforcing it has remained in the Comptroller. The number of corporations taxed in 1881 was 954, and the amount collected $1,539,864.27; the number in 1886 was 1,249, and the amount collected $1,239,864.16. In 1892 there were 1,780 corporations paying, and the amount collected was $1,430,719.86. In 1896 the number of corporations was 4,401, and the amount collected was $2,165,610.12. The amount of capital represented by these 4,401 corporations is believed to be fully $766,000,000.

Mr. Wadsworth gave place on January 1, 1882, to Ira Davenport, a capitalist and a Republican of Bath. Mr. Davenport had represented the twenty-seventh district in the State Senate in 1878, 1879, 1880 and 1881, and was elected Comptroller over G. H. Lapham. He was defeated for re-election as Comptroller by Alfred C. Chapin, November 6, 1883. In 1885, he received the Republican nomination for Governor, but was defeated by David B. Hill. He was a member of the Forty-ninth and Fiftieth Congresses. On March 1, 1883, the duty of auditing the canal accounts, after having been performed for thirty-five years by a separate officer—the Canal Auditor—was placed in the Comptroller's office, where it still remains. The confidence which the Republican party had shown in Comptroller Davenport was not misplaced. He was a man of high character and attainments, and performed the duties of the office of Comptroller with success.

Alfred C. Chapin, a lawyer and a Democrat, of Brooklyn, entered upon the discharge of his duties January 1, 1884. He was Member of Assembly from the eleventh Kings county district in 1882 and 1883, and in the latter year was chosen Speaker of that body. He was re-elected Comptroller in 1885 over Mr. Wadsworth. He has, since his service as Comptroller, served four years as Mayor of Brooklyn, from January 1, 1888, to January 1, 1892, and is now about ending a term as State Railroad Commissioner. In 1891, he was a prominent candidate for Governor before the Democratic convention, but was beaten by Roswell P. Flower. Mr. Chapin is an educated and cultivated gentleman, and as Comptroller was not afraid to run counter to established ideas. He strongly recommended, in a special message to the Legislature in 1885, and subsequently in his annual reports, the abolition of the common school fund, and its transfer to the treasury. By chapter 483 of the Laws of 1885, the Legislature laid a tax of five per cent upon collateral inheritances. This inaugurated a system of taxing transfers at death, which has come now to yield annually about $2,000,000. The Comptroller was largely intrusted with the duties of enforcing this law. It was amended in 1891 by making a tax of one per cent upon all direct inheritances. In 1886, the Comptroller was authorized to approve the bonds of banks designated as depositories of the funds of State institutions. The same year, the Comptroller was directed to make assessments on the various companies liable therefor to meet the expenses of the Subway Commissions in the cities of New York and Brooklyn—a duty which still rests on the office. In 1887, he was authorized to sell or exchange detached lands in certain counties of the Forest Preserve, upon the recommendation of the Forest Commission and the Attorney-General, the purpose being to consolidate the State's holding of lands in the Adirondack Park. The same year a tax was laid on racing associations for the benefit of agricultural societies to improve the breed of horses, etc., and the collection of this tax has since remained a part of the duty of the Comptroller, notwithstanding the various vicissitudes through which racing and pool bills have passed.

At the November election, in 1887, Edward Wemple was elected Comptroller over Jesse S. L'Amoreaux. Mr. Wemple was a manufacturer and Democrat, residing at Fultonville. He was a Member of Assembly from Montgomery county in 1877 and 1878, and a Member of the Forty-eighth Congress, but was defeated for re-election to that office by George West. He served in the State Senate from the eighteenth district in 1886 and 1887. He was re-elected Comptroller in 1889 over Martin W. Cooke.

In 1888 the Legislature passed an act requiring the agent and warden of each of the State prisons to file with the Comptroller a bond, approved by the Superintendent of State Prisons and Comptroller, in a penalty of not less than $50,000, to be fixed by the Comptroller. The same year the Legislature declared that the Board of Claims should have no jurisdiction over private claims required to be presented to the Comptroller for audit, until after his action on the claim. It further required all public officials and other persons receiving or disbursing moneys of the people of the State to deposit the same in some solvent bank or banking institution, to be designated by the Comptroller, and that every bank receiving such moneys should execute a bond to the people, to be filed with and approved by the Comptroller. By chapter 586 of the Laws of the same year the Comptroller, the Superintendent of State Prisons, and the President of the State Board of Charities, were constituted a board to fix the prices of all goods manufactured in the penal institutions of the State for the use of other State institutions. All these provisions of law are still in force, except that the board to fix prices has been changed by the addition of the State Prison Commission and Lunacy Commission, and by omitting the President of the State Board of Charities. In 1889 the right of the Comptroller to supervise the financial affairs of the prisons was enlarged, and the agent and warden required to make monthly reports of receipts and expenditures to him. He was also allowed to revise and readjust the accounts theretofore settled under the Corporation Tax

Law. In 1890 he was made a member of the "Board for the Establishment of State Insane Asylum Districts and other purposes," together with the State Commission in Lunacy and President of the State Board of Charities. In 1891 an act was passed requiring all institutions receiving moneys from the State treasury for maintenance, in full or in part, to deposit their funds in some responsible bank or banking house, to be designated by the Comptroller. He was also authorized to appoint commissioners to hear evidence and take proofs on applications for cancellation of title or redemption of lands.

On January 1, 1892, Frank Campbell, a banker and Democrat, of Bath, became Comptroller. He had been chosen in the previous election over Arthur C. Wade. He had held no office previous to that time. He served one term, ran for re-election in 1893 and was defeated. He has held no office since. By chapter 651 of the Laws of 1892 the supervision of the funds deposited in court was transferred from the General Term of the Supreme Court to the Comptroller, and this work the Comptroller's office has since performed; and by chapter 681 of the Laws of the same year he was required to approve all official undertakings.

In 1892 the authority was given to the Comptroller to license common carriers. He was relieved from this duty by the new Excise Law of 1896. By chapter 248 of the Laws of 1893 he, with the Secretary of State and Treasurer, was directed, before the first day of January of each year, to designate the State paper. The largest amount thus far collected in any one year under the Inheritance Tax Law was $3,071,687.09, in 1893, during Mr. Campbell's term. The amount collected under the Corporation Tax Law was increased during his term.

On January 1, 1894, James A. Roberts, a lawyer and Republican, of Buffalo, became Comptroller. He had served as Member of Assembly from the third district of Erie county in 1879, and from the fourth district of the same county in 1880. He was unanimously renominated from the fourth district in 1891, but declined. He was re-elected Comptroller in 1895 over John B. Judson. In 1894 the Comptroller was given power to appoint appraisers in cases of tuberculosis and glanders. In the same year the chancery fund, so called, which had been managed by the Clerk of the Court of Appeals after the abolition of the Court of Chancery, was turned over to the Comptroller. This fund, amounting to $169,935.52 in securities and cash, besides real estate of the possible value of $10,000, was the residue and remainder of moneys that had been deposited in the old Court of Chancery and never called for. By a rider on the appropriation bill of that year the superintendent or other managing officer of each State charitable institution or reformatory in the State was required to estimate monthly, in detail, the articles required by his institution for the ensuing month. The expenditures were to be limited to the estimates, and the treasurers were required to make monthly reports of their expenditures. This inaugurated substantially the same system, with reference to the expenditures of other charitable institutions, that was then used by the Lunacy Commission with reference to the hospitals. In 1895 this last provision was made more definite and explicit. The Comptroller was authorized the same year to appoint a second deputy, who was to have the same powers as the Deputy Comptroller. Twice before in the history of the office there had been a second deputy, but, after the continuance of the office for a few years, in each case it had been abolished. Chapter 79 of the Laws of 1895 provided for the issuing of canal bonds and created a sinking fund for their redemption. The issuing of the bonds and the care of the sinking fund were intrusted to the Comptroller. The same year the trustees of the Saratoga monument were authorized to transfer the property held by them to the State, and the Comptroller was made custodian of the monument.

While in the hundred years there have been thirty Comptrollers, there have been but eleven Deputy Comptrollers. Upon the passage of the act authorizing the appointment of a deputy, in 1811, Comptroller McIntyre appointed John Ely, Jr., and he held the position until 1822. He was succeeded by Ephraim Starr, who continued in the position until 1828. In 1828 Mr. Marcy appointed as deputy Philip Phelps, and, with the exception of two years, from February 28, 1840, to February 28, 1842, this being substantially the administration of Bates Cook, when the office was filled by W. W. Tredwell, Mr. Phelps held the place until 1876, or in all for forty-six years. It was long felt that his services were indispensable, and while Comptrollers might come and Comptrollers did go, the deputy seemed likely to go on forever. It is related that late in his official career he found himself growing footsore and lame, and no longer able to stand at his desk, as had been his custom, and scarcely able to reach the office, and there was talk of his resignation, and grave fears for the future finances of the State were expressed. In this emergency an attentive clerk found that the floor where the deputy had so long stood had been worn away so that an obdurate nail protruded, and it was standing upon this nail which had worked the woe. One blow of the hammer saved the State. Mr. Phelps was an able man, and his services in the office made him invaluable to the frequently-changing Comptrollers. At his death high testimonies to his worth and character were given by Sanford E. Church, Thomas Hillhouse, Wm. F. Allen, Robert H. Pruyn, John V. L. Pruyn, and many others. A meeting of State officers was held, at which Wm. Dorsheimer, then Lieutenant-Governor, presided, and resolutions expressing his great worth and service were adopted. It was well said that "no prospect of pecuniary advantage could swerve him from the strictest line of truth and justice."

Mr. Phelps was succeeded by Henry Gallien, who worthily filled the office from 1876 to 1884, when he died. Thomas E. Benedict held the office from 1884 to 1886. He has since been Deputy Secretary of State and Public Printer at Washington, and in all positions has acquitted himself as an able and upright man. Charles R. Hall succeeded to the office for a little more than a year, and was himself succeeded by Zerah S. Westbrook, who had the office for four years, from January 1, 1888, to January 1, 1892. Calvin J. Huson was Deputy Comptroller during Mr. Campbell's term. At the end of his term he was succeeded by Colonel William J. Morgan, who still holds the office.

The custom seems to have grown up in these degenerate times to make the term of the deputy co-terminous with that of Comptroller. This is of doubtful propriety. Too many men of tried integrity, familiar with their duties, cannot be retained in such an office. But the danger which would naturally be expected from a frequent change in both Comptroller and deputy has thus far been avoided by the retention, through succeeding administrations, of some of the most important clerks. Willis E. Merriman has now been in service in the Comptroller's office for thirty-one years, and, having worked up from the lowest to the highest service in the department, is familiar with all its details, and his services have thus become indispensable. Upon the creation of the office of Second Deputy Comptroller, in 1895, he was appointed to that position, and he has since discharged its duties with the fidelity and intelligence with which every Comptroller for many years has found him fortunately endowed.

No sketch of the office is complete without mention of George H. Birchall. He came into the office in 1883, at the time of the abolition of the Canal Auditor's office. He had served seventeen years in the last-named office. He has had charge of the canal accounts since their transfer to the Comptroller's office, and has rendered most efficient service. Messrs. Williams and Bliss came into the office in 1877, and Mr. Graham in 1882. Several employees have been in the department's service for six or eight years or more, and no department of the State government is better equipped with honest, faithful, public servants than is the Comptroller's office.

It can be seen from the foregoing that the duties of the Comptroller's office are varied and important. The boards of which he is a member give some indication of this fact. He is *ex-officio* a member of the State Board of Canvassers; of the Board of the Commissioners of the Land Office; of the Board of the Commissioners of the Canal Fund; of the Canal Board; of the State Commissioners of Charities; of the board to fix prices for prison made products; of the board for the establishment of State insane asylum districts, etc.; of the legislative printing board; of the department printing board, and one of the officers to designate the State paper. He manages the finances of the State so far even as to supervise the expenditures of the State institutions. He designates the banks in which funds of all institutions shall be deposited. He levies and collects the tax on corporations; supervises the collection of the transfer tax, and sells the lands of delinquent taxpayers in the counties in which are included a part of the Forest Preserve. He audits all accounts against the State; acts as a court in applications for cancellations of tax deeds or sales, and in disputed corporation tax matters; examines the court and trust funds deposited with the treasurer of every county in the State, and regulates the form of accounts and the manner of their investment, and performs many other less important duties too numerous for mention.

30th COMPTROLLER

Of the men who have held the office of Comptroller nineteen were lawyers; three were gentlemen farmers; three bankers; one a merchant; one a manufacturer; one a capitalist, and two were business men. In politics two were Federalists; fifteen Democrats (including under the word Democrats original Republicans, whether Clintonians or otherwise); four Whigs; two Anti-Masons; six Republicans, and one American or Know Nothing.

Deputy Comptroller, 46 Years.

The total expenditures of the State for each tenth year since the establishment of the office were as follows:

$$
\begin{array}{ll}
1797 & \$322{,}831\ 37 \\
1807 & 425{,}689\ 69 \\
1817 & 1{,}296{,}590\ 88 \\
1827 & 1{,}908{,}346\ 73 \\
1837 & 4{,}926{,}449\ 04 \\
1847 & 5{,}275{,}164\ 09 \\
1857 & 10{,}176{,}939\ 70 \\
1867 & 20{,}496{,}050\ 59 \\
1877 & {}^{[1]}26{,}186{,}744\ 70 \\
1887 & 16{,}771{,}448\ 98 \\
1897 & 26{,}510{,}425\ 77
\end{array}
$$

Each of these would very nearly represent the average annual expenditures for the decade which it ends.

The total expenditures of the National Government for the year 1797 were $8,625,877.37, and if we deduct from this the amounts paid for interest, and payments upon the public debt, it leaves the amount of ordinary expenditure but $2,836,110.52. The ordinary expenditures of the National Government did not reach the amount expended in this State for the year 1896 until the year 1847, if we except the years 1813, 1814 and 1815, when the expenditures were abnormal by reason of the War of 1812, and if we except also the years 1837 and 1838, and in none of those excepted years did the annual ordinary expenditures very greatly exceed this State's expenditure for 1896.

During the century, the State has expended for lands, construction, enlargement or permanent improvement:

Of its five canals	$74,347,000 00
Of its new Capitol	22,254,023 60
Of the twelve hospitals erected by it	$15,204,099 59
Of its seventeen other charitable institutions	6,369,110 70
Of its forty-five armories and arsenals	3,349,543 73
Of its three State prisons	4,528,058 65
Of its twelve normal schools	1,826,350 06
Making a total expenditure for those various purposes of	$127,878,186 33

Far the greater part of this money has been handled by, and drawn on the warrant of, the Comptroller, and no suspicion has ever arisen that this duty was not honestly performed. Nearly all of the sinking funds of the various bonded debts of the State have been managed by the Comptrollers, who, in these 100 years, have

[1] Includes $10,453,805.95 bounty debt.

never been the occasion of the loss of a single dollar.

2d Deputy Comptroller

Connected with the office 31 years

Jenkins, in his political history of New York, says that the Comptroller bears the same relation to the State that the Secretary of the Treasury does to the National Government, and this is largely true. I cannot do better in closing this brief sketch of the Comptroller's office than by quoting from Thurlow Weed's autobiography. His opportunities for, and keenness of, observation make his statement of peculiar value. He says: "It seems proper to say, amid all the mutations of party, and the liability under our form of popular government to occasionally find unworthy men elevated to high places, our State has ever been singularly fortunate in its highest financial officer. We have had unfaithful men in almost every other department of the State Government. We have had, in two or three instances, comparatively weak men in the office of Comptroller, but as a rule its incumbents have been capable, firm and incorruptible."

Lector House believes that a society develops through a two-fold approach of continuous learning and adaptation, which is derived from the study of classic literary works spread across the historic timeline of literature records. Therefore, we aim at reviving, repairing and redeveloping all those inaccessible or damaged but historically as well as culturally important literature across subjects so that the future generations may have an opportunity to study and learn from past works to embark upon a journey of creating a better future.

This book is a result of an effort made by Lector House towards making a contribution to the preservation and repair of original ancient works which might hold historical significance to the approach of continuous learning across subjects.

HAPPY READING & LEARNING!

LECTOR HOUSE LLP
E-MAIL: lectorpublishing@gmail.com